The Business Survival Guide

(because it's a jungle out there)

An Swinnen

The Business Survival Guide

(because it's a jungle out there)

ISBN: 978-1-4461-0107-0

Published by Lulu.com

Book cover design by Anthony Dolphin and Next Issue

Cartoons from www.cartoonstock.com

To everyone who has helped turn
BECS into a success

British

About the Author

An Swinnen is a Bachelor of Education and has worked in the British education system and English language schools. She has taught in primary, secondary, special needs, adult education and at Exeter University as a Senior Lecturer.

In 2004 An Swinnen set up Business English Consulting Service Ltd or BECS, a British training company that delivers tailor-made training worldwide. Major clients include Kuwait Petroleum Corporation, Qatargas, Aluminium Bahrain, Arab Open University, Bahrain Training Institute and the Belgian Government.

On 4 February 2011 An Swinnen was awarded the British Business Forum Excellence Award 2010 by Baroness Emma Nicholson for her achievements in Kuwait and the Gulf.

An Swinnen is often asked to speak at international conferences. In an informative and entertaining manner she covers different aspects of learning, education, business and export.

An Swinnen has accompanied the Crown Prince and Princess of Belgium on trade missions to Bahrain, Qatar, Saudi Arabia and Brazil and continues to do so.

Foreword

Over the last few years I have gone from a school teacher in South-West England to an award winning international business woman and author. How did I get there? How did I make the change from teaching thirty 11-year olds who did not want to learn French, into running my own company in Europe and the Middle East? Well, you have to use common sense, learn from your mistakes and listen to your friends.

First of all, you have to use common sense. To be successful in business you have to be professional, punctual, serious, hard-working and always look smart. It does not matter how frustrated you get, you have to stay friendly, polite and calm.

Secondly, you have to learn from your mistakes. I remember when the GPS-led taxi driver in Amsterdam took me on a sight-seeing tour instead of taking me to my meeting where I eventually turned up half an hour late with a big bill. Or the time where my transport to a business meeting in Kuwait consisted of four men on a bus and I briefly thought I was being kidnapped.

Thirdly, you learn from your friends. There have been so many people who have given me a lot of help and advice since I set up BECS; usually over dinner or a cup of coffee. To all of you, thank you. I would like to pass on my Business Survival Guide to you, as other people have done to me. Enjoy the book.

Contents

About the author p. 5

Foreword p. 7

Business Skills

Communication Skills p.17

Social Chit Chat p.19

Presentations p.21

PowerPoint Presentations p. 23

Negotiations p. 25

Telephoning p. 27

Meetings p. 29

Emails p. 31

Report Writing p. 33

Dealing with Complaints p. 35

Making a Complaint p. 37

Management Skills

Be a Good Boss p. 41

Leadership p. 43

Team Building p. 45

Organising Skills p. 47

Running your Business

Your Corporate Image p. 51

Sales and Marketing p. 53

Increase Sales: Export p. 55

Websites p. 57

Newsletters p. 59
Free Publicity p. 61
Free Help p. 63
Funding p. 65
Do not be Afraid to Ask p. 67
Trade Missions p. 69
Trade Fairs and Exhibitions p. 71
Love your Competitors p. 73
Getting Appointments p. 75
Winning Business p. 77
Getting Paid p. 79
Keeping your Costs Down p. 81
Dealing with Agents p. 83
Contracts p. 85
Training p. 87
Problem Solving p. 89
Circumstances Beyond Your Control p. 91

Social Skills
Be Nice p. 95
Business Travel p. 97
Taxi Drivers p. 99
Staying at Hotels p. 101
Business and Food p. 103
Money Abroad p. 105
Business Women p. 107
Cultural Differences p. 109
Business Etiquette p. 111
Networking p. 113

Facebook p. 115
Following the News p. 117
Dealing with Stress p. 119
Enjoying Life p. 121
Useful Website Addresses p. 123

More about BECS p. 124
Feedback from Clients p. 126
Conferences p. 127
Contact Details p. 129

Business Skills

"OUR SPAM WILL CONTACT YOUR SPAM..."

Communication Skills

1. Speak slowly and clearly.

2. Do not use complicated words or words only used in your company.

3. Do not rely on spoken communication if you want to give a group of people the same information because the content will change from person to person. Send an email, letter or memo instead.

4. If you are not sure if you understood the message, ask for repetition or ask for an explanation.

5. Do not be afraid to ask for clarification several times. Do not stop until you have understood because the consequences could be terrible (dangerous situation, missed flight, wrong medication…)

"Enough small talk. It's time for big talk."

Social Chit Chat

1. When you welcome visitors, ask about their journey, if they have been to the city before, discuss the weather (UK) or ask where they come from (USA).

2. Never discuss politics or religion.

3. Social chit chat makes you feel at ease so relax and enjoy the conversation.

4. If you run out of things to talk about, look around and start talking about what you see (the furniture, pictures on the walls, the view).

5. Your host will move on to business when he/she is ready. Do not change the subject to business yourself.

Before Powerpoint.

Presentations

1. Allow plenty of time for preparation. The more you prepare, the less nervous you will be.

2. Check the equipment before you start your presentation.

3. Structure your presentation into introduction, body, conclusion and questions.

4. Use simple language and speak slowly and clearly.

5. Establish a relationship with the audience through eye contact and by asking questions.

...and as you can clearly see from this chart, I haven't got the slightest idea how to use PowerPoint.

Streeter

PowerPoint Presentations

1. Keep it simple.

2. Use a lot of images and very little text.

3. Do not stand with your back to the audience when you look at the screen.

4. Do not read out the text. Your audience can read.

5. Use subtle animation. You do not want your audience to have epileptic fits because of flashing and fast-moving images.

"Now's a good time to get a feel for your negotiating skills."

Negotiations

1. Prepare before the negotiation and know what you want.

2. Always stay polite and calm.

3. Give the other party compliments e.g. "You have an excellent reputation and we would like to work with you."

4. Use "we" and "us" instead of "you" e.g. "How can we solve the problem?" instead of "How are you going to solve the problem?"

5. Clarify and confirm throughout the negotiations e.g. "So what you are saying is…is that correct?"

"I won't be taking any more calls today. I threw my phone out the window."

Telephoning

1. Smile while you dial. The other person will hear the smile in your voice.

2. Introduce yourself slowly at the beginning of a call. The receiver needs to register who you are before you can give them more information.

3. Never shout at an operator, especially if they need to help you because your file will go to the bottom of the pile.

4. Spell information slowly and use examples e.g. N for November.

5. Always thank the other person at the end of a call e.g. “Thank you for your help” or “Thank you for phoning”.

MEETING ROOM
REASONS IT'S NOT YOUR FAULT
4 FOR $1.00
DaveCarpenter...

Meetings

1. The chair person is the most important person at the meeting. He/she should listen, direct the meeting, summarize and conclude at the end.

2. Do not be afraid to say something at a meeting. You might have the best idea.

3. Be on time so you can finish on time.

4. Take your own notes so you do not have to wait for the minutes to be published.

5. Stick to the agenda and do not start talking about issues that are not important at that time.

GOOD MORNING. YOU HAVE TWELVE MILLION TERABYTE UNREAD E-MAILS.
PIERO TONIN

Emails

1. Do not send an email to your whole contact list unless you really have to. Otherwise people will stop reading your emails altogether. If you have to send to all your contacts, paste them into the BCC box so you keep email addresses private.

2. Make sure that your subject is memorable so people open and read your email (not “hello”).

3. Never write anything negative about a person. Eventually it will come back to haunt you.

4. Embarrassing emails can travel around the world within a few hours so be careful.

5. Check who you are sending the email to before you “reply to all”.

WE'RE TRYING TO ENCOURAGE STAFF TO BE MORE CREATIVE IN THEIR REPORT WRITING...
I CALL THIS MY DANCE OF THE FOURTH QUARTERS CLIENT SATISFACTION SURVEY...
FRAN

Report Writing

1. Use short and easy sentences. The easier to read the better.

2. Most people do not read the whole report so focus on the executive summary which people will read.

3. Make the report look attractive with colours, graphics, photographs and other visual tools.

4. Make sure there is enough white space on a page so the text does not look too busy. People get tired quickly looking at a lot of words on one piece of paper.

5. Use headings, subheadings, colours, bullet points, sequencing, underlining, italics and fonts to make your report more readable.

"Now, what's your complaint?"

Dealing with Complaints

1. Always stay calm and polite.

2. Try to calm the other party down.

3. If you are not at fault, explain the situation and say "I regret any inconvenience that may have arisen", then help the client.

4. Listen to the complaint without interrupting. Write down the questions you would like to ask later.

5. Always tell the complainant what you are going to do next to try and solve the problem so they know you are doing something to help.

"…. Further to our telephone conversation of the 3rd, my fax of the 11th, my letters of the 16th, 23rd and 28th, my e-mails of… ……."

Making a Complaint

1. Never shout at or be rude to the Customer Service Agent. They are usually not at fault.

2. Have all the details with you (invoices, receipts, reference numbers).

3. Stay calm and polite.

4. If you feel that the Customer Service Agent does not know how to proceed, politely ask for the Manager.

5. Thank Customer Service at every stage for their help. You will achieve so much more as people want to help nice customers.

Management Skills

YOUR TURN NEXT!
FRAN
1
WE WANT EVERYONE TO BE NUMBER ONE

Be a Good Boss

1. Treat your staff well and they will do anything for you.

2. Happy staff turns up for work.

3. Listen to your staff.

4. Do not forget to thank your staff for their good work.

5. Celebrate birthdays, special events and occasions.

THE GOOD NEWS IS THAT YOU'LL BE LEADING THE TEAM...
AND THE BAD NEWS?
YOU ARE THE TEAM!
FRAN.

Leadership

1. Know your strong and weak points.

2. Know the strong and weak points of the people in your team.

3. Greet your team in the morning.

4. Listen actively to your team.

5. Do not ignore problems within your team and hope they will go away. They will not. Deal with them as soon as possible.

"They can't work as a team."

Team Building

1. The team needs to agree on a strategy before you start a task.

2. Organize team building time with your team, e.g. cake meetings, breakfasts, …

3. Give each other compliments and rewards when the team does well.

4. Support each other in difficult times.

5. Good communication is vital. Make sure every one knows what is happening.

LOGISTICS
DEPARTMENT
PENS
PAPER
PLAN
A
PAPER
B
PENS
C
TO ME
CHAFF.

Organising Skills

1. Know what you want to achieve so you can work towards it. These include personal and professional achievements. (setting up your own business, starting a family).

2. Use time planners such as your mobile phone or diaries such as the WH Smith diaries (see www.whsmith.co.uk).

3. Make lists of things you need to do. Crossing them off gives you a satisfying feeling of achievement.

4. Get the balance work-free time right. Do not forget to enjoy life.

5. Eat healthily. Eat brain foods that help you concentrate such as vegetables, nuts, oily fish and so on.

Running your Business

"Yes, you are speaking to grandma."

Your Corporate Image

1. Look professional through your brochures, business cards and website.

2. What image would you like to portray? Make sure it fits your address. Have a virtual address in London if you would like to impress. Do not use “flat” addresses.

3. Always use “we” and “us” when you discuss your company instead of “I” and “me”.

4. Make sure you score high on large search engines such as Yahoo and Google. See my websites tips.

5. Have a company profile on www.linkedin.com. They will register your website on large search engines for free.

"Relax. I'm not selling."

Sales and Marketing

1. Always dress smartly because you are the front of the company you represent.

2. Send out a newsletter. You can find free software on the internet such as Email Marketing Pro. See my Newsletter tips.

3. In a first meeting do not focus too much on PowerPoint presentations. Concentrate on establishing a relationship with the potential client instead.

4. Always send a follow-up email thanking the potential client for the good meeting.

5. Stay in touch with them, even when they do not put in an order immediately.

"If you want produce grown on the farm down the road you'll have to go to Kuala Lumpur."

Increase Sales: Export

1. Research if there is a market for your product abroad.

2. Go on an international trade mission to see if there is a need for your product.

3. Business agencies such as UK Trade and Investment will advise you for free and have special export schemes.

4. Your embassy will help you. Contact them before your visit.

5. Translate your website and brochures into the target language.

"Good afternoon, gentlemen, and welcome to multi.global.industries.com... otherwise known as my basement."

Websites

1. Make sure your website looks professional. It is your “shop window”.

2. Update your website regularly.

3. Have a “news” section so people can see the company is still active.

4. Use a lot of images and little text.

5. Web’s Biggest (www.websbiggest.com) will rank your website high on the large search engines. Choose their “Search Engine Submission Service” which is excellent and very cheap.

THE COMPANY NEWSLETTER

"AND FINALLY, THIS MONTH WE'LL FEATURE EACH USER'S EVERY MOVE, RECORDING CHAT ROOM TRANSCRIPTS, INSTANT MESSAGES, E-MAILS SENT OR RECEIVED, AND ALL WEBSITES VISITED ! "

Newsletters

1. Send a newsletter to your contact list every three months or when there is some news.

2. Keep the newsletter short and easy to read.

3. Have a link at the bottom so people can subscribe or unsubscribe.

4. Email Marketing Pro is excellent newsletter software which can be downloaded for free from www.emailmarketingprofessional.com.

5. A newsletter keeps your name in the limelight.

"This is strictly off the record...."

Free Publicity

1. Word of mouth advertising is the best advertising in the world. Ask your clients to recommend you.

2. Contact the press when there is some company news.

3. You can publish your news, PowerPoints and other documents on www.linkedin.com.

4. Write articles for magazines (local, trade, association, etc) or newspapers.

5. Many directories have free listings.

"And never forget that the best things in life are freebies."

Free Help

1. Citizens Advice gives you free help and information.

2. Find a relevant group or forum on the internet and ask the question. You might want to check the 'free' answer.

3. Professionals such as accountants and solicitors usually offer a free first session.

4. Your Bank Manager and Financial Advisors offer free financial advice.

5. Government-funded business agencies such as Business Link and UKTI offer help and funding to entrepreneurs and companies.

I'M HERE TO ASK YOU FOR FUNDING FOR MY FURTHER DEVELOPMENT.
PIERO TONIN

Funding

1. Business Link, UKTI and Chambers of Commerce have funding schemes available. Check with them.

2. You can find funding and grants on www.grantfinder.co.uk.

3. Funding for training might be available at your local college or university.

4. Google "funding" and your sector, area or project and see what comes up.

5. Go to your local library and ask the assistant for help.

OK.. IF I CAN'T FIND MY WAY BACK TO MY CUBICLE IN 2 MORE DAYS, I'LL DEFINITELY CONSIDER ASKING FOR HELP.

Do Not be Afraid to Ask

1. "No" you have, "yes" you can get.

2. Ask for help when you need it.

3. Ask your clients and friends to recommend you.

4. Ask your clients and friends if they know if anyone needs your services or products.

5. Ring up a company and ask the operator for names, telephone numbers and email addresses of people you would like to talk to.

John couldn't help but think that his team had a different perspetive on the event than he did ....

Trade Missions

1. Trade missions are an excellent way of researching and entering a new market.

2. International trade missions are organised by Chambers of Commerce, business groups and embassies.

3. Give the organisers a list of the people and companies you would like to see and they will organise a meeting.

4. The organisers will also organise networking events such as lunches, receptions and balls. Go to them.

5. You not only get to know potential clients and agents at trade missions, but also your competition.

"Rent an auditorium and charge $39.95 a seat. Thank you for coming."

Trade Fairs and Exhibitions

1. Exhibiting at trade fairs is very expensive.

2. Only exhibit if you can afford it.

3. Go to a trade fair as a visitor to see what is happening in your field.

4. Take enough business cards with you and hand them out to people you meet.

5. You find a list of trade fairs and exhibitions by industry, by country, by date, by venue, by organiser on www.biztradeshows.com.

" I REALLY WISH THE LANDLORD HAD NEVER RENTED THE FLOOR ABOVE US TO ONE OF OUR COMPETITORS."

Love Your Competitors

1. It is very important that you know who your competitors are. Look at their websites and see what they offer.

2. Competitors are in a good position to help you because they know the market.

3. Work together and not against each other.

4. Get together regularly to discuss innovations, changes, new laws, etc.

5. Never criticise your competitors to clients. It is very unprofessional.

"Helen, it looks like you can cancel my 2:15"

Getting appointments

1. Try to get introduced to potential clients.

2. Find out who you need to speak to. If you do not know, ask the company's operator.

3. Always mention in the beginning of a telephone call or email how you got their details.

4. Simply ask for a meeting.

5. Always include your contact details and website address in an email.

"Now think, Harris, what did you do different on that day?"

Winning Business

1. Get yourself on the approved supplier list of companies.

2. Send a professional proposal that is easy to read and looks attractive.

3. Send your proposal in PDF and not Microsoft Word format.

4. Make a follow-up phone call after a few days if you have not heard anything.

5. If you do not get the contract, find out why and learn from this.

"I'm putting you in charge of past due accounts."

Getting Paid

1. If you can, demand 100% of the invoice upfront. Especially if you have to travel for the work or if it means a big investment on your part.

2. The next best thing is 50% or more upfront.

3. If they will not pay upfront, check your client's reputation and financial situation.

4. You can check your client's reputation and financial situation by asking them for a reference, through your bank, Google, embassies or Companies House.

5. Do not be afraid to go to the top if you do not get paid.

"I'M STILL EMPLOYED, BUT TO SAVE ON UTILITY COSTS, THEY OFFSHORED ME."

Keeping Your Costs Down

1. Compare suppliers' prices (phone, electricity, printer's, etc) and see if it is worth switching.

2. Set up a virtual office and work from home or share an office.

3. Travel economy.

4. Do not be afraid to haggle. Your suppliers want to keep your custom.

5. Use Skype (www.skype.com), MSN Messenger (www.msn.com) or Yahoo Messenger (www.yahoo.com) to make free telephone calls.

OF COURSE I TRUST MY AGENT... HE'S GOT TWO VERY HONEST FACES.
CONSULTANT

Dealing with Agents

1. Avoid signing a MOU (Memorandum of Understanding) because of international agent's laws, unless you have worked together successfully for several years.

2. Never sign a MOU with someone you have only just met. You do not know this person!

3. Do not sign a MOU with a newly established company. They do not have a network yet.

4. Sign project-per-project agreements instead.

5. There are agents who "collect" high-profile companies. They will sign you up and move on to the next one without doing anything for you.

"The fine print, in the contract, can be read only if held up to a mirror."

Contracts

1. Ask a solicitor to look at your sample contracts.

2. Always have contracts for all your staff all the time.

3. Have a contract for each project you do.

4. Ask a solicitor to look at contracts agents, clients or suppliers would like you to sign.

5. If you can not afford a solicitor, ask a legal charity such as Citizens Advice (www.citizensadvice.org.uk) and they will help you for free.

"Okay...tell me again what training seminar we sent Bill to?"

Training

1. Training means investing in yourself and your people.

2. You never stop learning.

3. Both internal and external company training is important.

4. Make sure that your training company does not outsource the work to a low-quality company.

5. Do not forget to read. You learn a lot from reading newspapers, magazines, books and the internet.

PROBLEM SOLVING
THEORY
PRACTICE
PAY
HERE
NAYLOR

Problem Solving

1. There are always several solutions to a problem.

2. Ask others how they would solve the problem.

3. Look at all the factors before making a decision.

4. Do not be afraid to ask for help.

5. The problem might go away so do not get too stressed.

WATCH
THIS SPACE
Roy Delgado

Circumstances Beyond Your Control

1. You are not responsible for circumstances beyond your control.

2. Do your best, that is all you can do.

3. Relax, sit back and see what happens.

4. Have plan B ready.

5. Do not be afraid to stop and move on if nothing happens.

Social Skills

"Mr Frimley, sir, can I have a word about the motivational artwork..."

Be Nice

1. Be nice, polite and respectful. You are treated the way you treat others.

2. A smile can do wonders (especially if you need other drivers to let you in).

3. Pay someone a compliment. You will make that person's day.

4. Do not lie. Lies are found out eventually.

5. Do not cheat. You might win in the short term but you will lose your reputation.

EXPORT
MANAGER
LAS
VEGAS
BALI
RIO
MORRIS

Business Travel

1. Use internet search engines such as www.opodo.com to look for good deals on flights.

2. Check in online if you can so you save time at the airport.

3. Arrange an airport-hotel transfer with your hotel. You will save time not queuing for a taxi and it is nice to see a friendly face waiting for you. Hotel representatives can also help if there are any problems such as missing luggage.

4. Always ask a taxi driver how much the fare will be before you get in.

5. Beware of taxi drivers who rely on GPS.

"Where does he think he is - Wall Street?"

Taxi drivers

1. Always use official licensed taxis.

2. Ask beforehand how much the fare will be. If there is a meter, ask for an approximate price.

3. Always ask if they know where the address is before you get in the taxi.

4. Do not use dirty taxis that look as if they are going to break down.

5. Always use a seat belt. If there is no seat belt at the back, sit in the front.

"Room service, sir. You wanted someone to listen to your speech for the banker's dinner."

Staying at Hotels

1. Make use of all the hotel facilities. The business lounges are great places to have meetings.

2. Use internet search engines such as www.booking.com to look for good deals on hotels.

3. Concierges are wonderful people who can act as your Personal Assistant.

4. Be nice to receptionists. They can get you other rooms and late check-outs.

5. Be nice to housekeeping staff. They provide you with the free goodies. They also look after things you might forget in the room.

"Are you the client, or am I?"

Business and Food

1. The host decides how much you are going to eat: starter-main meal-dessert. Follow their example.

2. Choose something easy to eat (not spaghetti bolognese or reception food that falls apart when you touch it).

3. Wait for your host to start talking about business.

4. Don't drink too much alcohol.

5. The host pays the bill. Thank him again for the meal in a follow-up email or text.

"Okay, she's got her card in, now shut it down."

Money Abroad

1. Tell your bank that you are travelling abroad. Otherwise they might block your card when you try to use it. If this happens contact your bank.

2. Change some money before you travel. Some airports do not have cash machines.

3. Always have some cash on you in case of emergencies. Make sure you always have enough cash to get a taxi to your embassy if necessary.

4. Do not get stressed if a cash machine does not give you the money you have asked for, even if the machine has the visa logo.

5. Find a large international bank such as HSBC, Barclays, etc and try again.

IT DIDN'T HELP WHEN YOU TOLD HER SHE LOOKED BEAUTIFUL WHEN SHE WAS ANGRY
Ms STEELE
MANAGING DIRECTOR

Business Women

1. In the same way that men dress to impress, wear an elegant business dress in meetings instead of a trouser suit. It works!

2. Do not wear flat shoes but do not wear very high heels either.

3. Wear a little make-up.

4. Do not look too sexy. People will look at you but will not listen to what you have to say.

5. As a woman you stand out and it will be easier for you to get appointments. You have an advantage over men. Use it.

"The shareholders want more cultural diversity. Choose a si-man, hai-man, and ja-man to replace three yes-men."

Cultural Differences

1. Read up on cultural differences before you go to a foreign country or when a foreigner joins your team. It will prevent embarrassing situations. You can find a lot of information in libraries and on the internet.

2. We are all different. Do not be afraid but learn from others. When in Rome, do as the Romans do e.g. cover your shoulders in the Middle East, only use your right hand in India, and do not use a handkerchief in public in Japan.

3. Cultural differences might also mean communication problems. When someone from China says "Yes" it means "I have understood", not "I agree".

4. Make sure you do not break any laws, e.g. you can not kiss or hug in public in Muslim countries. If you get into trouble, contact your Embassy.

WAP!
GODDARD

Business Etiquette

1. Do not ignore emails and voice mails. Always answer them, even to let people know you do not have the information they need.

2. Do not cancel a meeting by text a few hours beforehand. Telephone to apologise and explain why you can not make the meeting.

3. Do not break any promises you have made. If you need to and it is beyond your control, telephone people to explain.

4. Be punctual. If you are going to be late (traffic jam, flight delay) let your contact know.

5. Dress appropriately. If you are not sure what the dress code is, check beforehand.

"Mr Longman, which do you think would help me more in my career - a course on accountancy or some golf lessons?"

Networking

1. Never eat alone. Join someone's table or arrange to eat with your colleagues, friends, boss.

2. Always carry business cards with you and hand them out so people can get in touch with you.

3. Linkedin (www.linkedin.com) is a fantastic website which lets you network with the world for free.

4. Do not drink too much alcohol at social events because it does not look professional.

5. Ask your friends or colleagues if they know someone who can be of interest to you. They will be happy to help and introduce you.

"Your MBA and PhD degrees are impressive but what concerns me is your low number of Facebook friends."

Facebook

1. Have your security settings very high unless you would like 1000 friends.

2. Do not put photos or comments on Facebook that can be embarrassing for yourself or others.

3. Comments on "walls" can be seen by others so think twice before you write.

4. Do not spend too much time on Facebook because it looks as if you do not have anything else to do.

5. Do not play Facebook games such as "FarmVille". Use the time to grow your own business instead.

"I can get the latest market news from the New York stock exchange."

Following the News

1. Keep updated. The news is often discussed before or after meetings.

2. You will find out what is happening in the world and how it affects your business.

3. Do not travel to dangerous areas. Check with your embassy before making travel arrangements. Also check www.fco.gov.uk.

4. You will learn new things.

5. Reading opens up the world and its opportunities to you.

STRESS MANAGEMENT
BOB'S RELAXATION CLASSES SEEM TO HAVE WORKED!
SUNEXTREME
ARCHER
UNA PALOMA BLANCA

Dealing with Stress

1. Leave the office and go outside. Have a coffee in your favourite café, go shopping or go for a walk.

2. Exercise. Sport helps you clear your mind and is healthy.

3. Go to a church/mosque/temple/quiet place where material problems are easily forgotten and you can see the bigger picture.

4. Have a long, hot bath.

5. Drink camomile tea.

"But on the positive side, money can't buy happiness - so who cares?"

Enjoying life

1. Eat and drink with your family and friends.

2. Think of what you have, not of what you do not have.

3. Life is short. Enjoy every day as if it is your last.

4. Make time for your hobbies.

5. Live healthily so you can enjoy life to the full.

Useful Website Addresses

LinkedIn	www.linkedin.com
Google	www.google.com
Yahoo	www.yahoo.com
MSN	www.msn.com
Skype	www.skype.com
Facebook	www.facebook.com
Opodo	www.opodo.com
Booking.com	www.booking.com
Web's Biggest	www.websbiggest.com
Business Link	www.businesslink.gov.uk
UK Trade and Investment	www.uktradeinvest.gov.uk
Companies House	www.companieshouse.gov.uk
Foreign and Commonwealth Office	www.fco.gov.uk
Email Marketing Pro	www.emailmarketingprofessional.com
Biz Tradeshows	www.biztradeshows.com
Grant Finder	www.grantfinder.co.uk
Citizens Advice	www.citizensadvice.org.uk
WH Smith	www.whsmith.co.uk
Cartoon Stock	www.cartoonstock.com
BECS	www.becsltd.com

More about BECS

BECS Training

- Business Skills Training (Soft Skills)
- Management Training
- Train the Trainer
- LCCI and EDI Qualifications

Why choose BECS?

We provide tailor-made solutions for your training needs. The client decides on:

- Course Content and Objectives
- Course Duration
- Course Location
- Follow-up

Our courses are fun

We use different methods to show that training is not just theory, for example:

- BBC series and films
- Interactive projects
- Games
- Quizzes

Excellent consultants

We have a small team of hand-picked consultants with a business and management background. All our trainers are experienced and qualified professionals who realize that English is a second language for our students. Our trainers are the guides to success which shows in the official course feedback given at the end of the course.

BECS Training Locations

- In-Company Training Worldwide
- BECS Training Centre on the English Riviera
- BECS Training Centre in London

www.becsltd.com

info@becsltd.com

Feedback from Clients

"The Microsoft Excel course in Paignton was organized very well at late notice. Richard Crowther was an excellent consultant who taught me a lot in just two days. I strongly recommend BECS for future training."

Christian Mouvet, Embassy of Belgium in London

"The contents of this report writing course were great. We had the chance to learn new techniques that can help us in the future. The instructor was very knowledgeable and was able to deliver the information smoothly despite the fact that all participants had different levels. The facilities were great and the visual aids were fantastic. I would definitely recommend this course to my colleagues or simply anyone willing to improve their report writing."

Yaser Alnami, Kuwait Petroleum Corporation

"The communication course was excellent. I enjoyed it and felt I learnt a lot. The tutor was giving us a lot of practical guidance. Furthermore, what was particularly pleasing was that she was very sensitive to the fact that our teaching situation is different. I would certainly recommend that our company sends some one on the course again next time."

Fawaz Al-Zafiri, Kuwait Oil Company

Conferences

An Swinnen is regularly asked to speak at conferences as an Education and Training Expert. She also speaks at conferences targeting graduates and aspiring entrepreneurs.

In an informative and entertaining manner An covers:

- Top Tips on how to learn more and become more efficient and successful
- Different aspects of training and education
- What you should really know to succeed in international business
- Top Tips for graduates and aspiring entrepreneurs

If you would like to book An as a Speaker, email her on info@becsltd.com

Contact Details

Address UK

Business English Consulting Service Ltd

126 Aldersgate Street

London EC1A 4JQ

UK

Tel. +44 7811960289

Address Kuwait

Business English Consulting Service Ltd

PO Box 36213

Salmiya 24753

Kuwait

Tel. +965 60042473

Tel. Brussels +32 478014201

Tel. Abu Dhabi +971 552039017

www.becsltd.com

info@becsltd.com

www.ingramcontent.com/pod-product-compliance
Ingram Content Group UK Ltd.
Pitfield, Milton Keynes, MK11 3LW, UK
UKHW020126250726
13967UKWH00002B/508

9 781446 101070